GALOS; Z J

ATHENS ELEGIES

BOOK I
DAY 1 TO DAY 7
BOOK II
DAY 8 TO DAY 16

A POET'S LAMENT

Lyric Poetry

Impressum

Bibliographical Information of the German Nation-
al Library.
The German National Library indexes this publica-
tion with the German National Bibliography. De-
tailed biographical data may be derived from the
Internet website http://dnb.dnb.de

©2020 GALOS; Z J
Producer and publisher: BoD-Books on Demand,
Norderstedt.
Artwork: ZG'14 'A Blue Love'

ISBN: 9783751904360

BOOK I
DAYS 1 to 7

1
THE DAY OF ARRIVAL

The winged air ship's body
Had landed soft-footed and
Then rolled onto the land of
My ancestral home, the land
Where all Western culture
Stems from.
I had joy in my heart and a tear
Welled in my right eye
For I did seek a beloved to
Stand and be there when the
Doors bi-parted and I would
Emerge within the masses of
Milling people who also seek
Someone
Who'll take them into his arms
And human warmth will well
Deep inside and spread in a
Rush of vibes that could be felt
Even by those

Who stand around and about
This early time of morn'
When the crack of dawn
Ca still be seen on the eastern
Horizon
As a sure appearance for another
Sunlit day, and we, who have sailed
Above the clouds all night
Now sweep along the highways
Into the city's bowl and wonder
About the crystal clear face of the
Temple-the grand old temple-
That'll shine into our room
Well-lit and defined
The white knight in his shining
Marble's armour, or hers, as it is
At least a woman's triumph
That has reverberated all around
Planet Earth.
This is the time I feel her presence
Although I know she'll sleep and rest
And I am here to love her, console her
And give her all I have to give and
Much more.
Even more, so much that it'll not
Spoil this love,
Whatever happens,
But then there's love besides
Compassion
Besides the way the cookie

Crumbles.
And then what will anybody say?
It's too early to speculate about
All scenarios and the voices are
Attached to such findings
Besides, I wish sometimes
We would be caught in the
Act of love, as I have dreamt
About.
But such just emerging thoughts
Are here to be written about
Here to be speculated about
In the lands
Love had the proper expressions
Of people to love and to be all
Together in Love at times of
Celebrations
When group-sex was called:
Symposium.
And now we are all civilized and
Yet we yearn for some adventure
Some unusual thing to happen
That drives us wild, or to the
Edge
To test our human conscious
Existence.
And here I am ringing the doorbell
And enter to her place: Ne?
And slip up the marbled stair and
Fall into the hands of her spouse

Who greets me with a brotherly
Hug's hello and then I kiss the
Woman I desire
The one I loved and love and still
Want to be with
Almost more than just formally
Married
More than just a sexual buddy
One I love to do it with
One who gave me everything she
Had inside and screwed me so
Intensely.
One who I desired so much that
Lewd thoughts came about when
We just touched
Whenever she gave herself totally
To the motions of my dedicated
Lovemaking.

And now as I take her out and
Drive her to the place of her desired
Electronic needs that give her an
Edge over her illness
An edge to her everyday life that
Now as I have arrived
I will have to nurture with her
Together
Nurture like my love she slowly
Feels
And then will come to react upon

Even if delayed or with less fear
Of being known to her spouse and
Family.
She has that eeriness of slow-mo.
And that is due to her habit
Changing infusions that are due
Every week once
But now she's got another three
Day's grace on top
Three days in which there' no
Chemistry
But solely the overlaying one from
Me
And I know I have to be the only
Patient
Her deep reactions are due to
Come.

I want to be with her. Oh Aleta,
Ana, Anetha, my Muse that has
Like a flower welted a bit in the
Dryness of her suffered times
Since the day of discoveries
Digging deep into her fragile being
Something rare and unexpected
Immediate
And like a dark cloud that spun
Itself into the clearness of the
Skies
Between a radiant young sun and

A clear and polished azure-blue of
Stones
Rising majestically and high into
The endless skies of eyes
Into desires deep in you –
These rays of my awakening
That lied unused and fallow in the
Grooves of cold and dusky nights
Of dryness
Suffocating in their overflowing
Lust of tremors and shakings
Like an abandoned child in storms
Of puberty and fevers of his bod's
Shivers
Shaking of skins
Burning in its own fires of
Self-absorption and deep fried lust
That has on the tongues of Sirens
Tasted as delicious cum
Juices from a burning body of grapes
Wine from the lap of gods and life
To be tasted and sipped
Drunk to the sounds of sweet
Slurping.
And then the first kiss that comes
Naturally and wanted as soon as
There is some space of confidentiality
And the loneliness of two pulsing
Bodies that swill
Like new-found hearts together

In the sweet stickiness of time
That has them embroiled in a fast
And fleeting kiss.
Ah! The first tasting
The first touches
Skin and back now partly bare
Lie on the sliding of his palm
And the sighs from her lips that part
And desire- like his lips – the unfolding
Of her dried-out body
That slowly steps into this
Third-time-cycle of love again
Now and then again
And all the fears have been beaten
Back.
There's the font that had dried-up
And the spring that has started
Flowing again
The trickle that broke the surface
Of the ivory sand and
The leathery crust of the earth
Keeping the tongue wet and the body
Cooled down from the fires of sweet
Waters
That emerge from her body
A spring from her eyes that flows
Across her lips
And spreads onto her breasts
Trickling down her belly and further
To her warm welcoming thighs.

He loves her
This poet of erotic senses:
I LOVE HER. ILOVE HER...
He repeats like a chorus deep in
His heart.
And when he rushes back to his base
Below the precipice of the
SACRED ROCK
He listens to his heart beat...
I have arrived at my ISLAND OF LOVE
I know now.
It does not matter if we had had so many
Sleepless nights and painful hours
We are together again
At last!

2
THE SECOND DAY (Monday)

Once I had met her, touched her, felt
Her presence, even if slightly detached
The first day
Yet the coals of love that had endured
Many lonesome hours and
The yearnings in a stealthy love
That might be almost sensed by our
Closest dependents
It's nethertheless building up
Tensions of desires and a want of lust
Still to be had

To be still yearned for in this condition
Of a jet-lagged seasoned traveler and
His beloved friend and Muse
His best confidant and greatest love
Someone he has only to touch
To spread the spark of lust inside
Into the flame that will draw itself into
His own and melt and fuse
And like a moth seeks the candle
Of his lust
That will turn him into ashes
In his lascivious ways that thrill him
With her together
Again and again and
Ever let go
Never fade
Until they will die in small little
Deaths together
In small exhilarated bursts of
Explosions inside
In Greek Fires they have lit
And are prepared to consume
Again and again.
This is the time of life, not death,
Not yet, never will, never dies.

There was a sign and a bell and
Then the message appeared:
Where are you my love, where?
I responded deeply stirred
Almost like a man who has a woman
He cannot do without
But to see her daily and like from
A spring

To sip the water of youth.
I sprang away as a deer that had
Been stirred by the hunter
Who had broken the twigs below
His tiring feet
Which had lost control for just a
Moment
For just one time he left his life
To become a story with a life
Of its own
He thrives on tensions of the
Unexpected.

I hurry out of the peach-coloured
Room and along the carpeted passage
That takes the impact from my
Rubber-soled shoes
And I hurry down the steps of this
Ship of fools
Into the part that lets me enter into
The streets of downtown Athens
The marble-paved boulevards
The elegant Classical-styled houses
Passed the Foundation of Onassis
And the ever young and frozen
Melina
Everybody knows
Even if you are only Greek in your
Mind.
The dog at the corner has eyes
That can judge the people
Who approach its natural domain
Without a blink of its eyelids.

The woman who occupies a seat
In front of the shop
She sells the schlock to tourists
Is friendly
Recognizing my accent immediately
And speaking some words in a
Cape-Dutch dialect.
Now I see the fire in her eyes has
Not yet extinguished like the seasons
And not yet cold like mornings in May
Still are.
I pass Melina's unfortunate bust and
Greet her my way
With a kiss she must appreciate
As a sensual woman
Then stride along the part I do enjoy –
Walking across the double-bank road:
Syngrou with the traffic giant of a lion
Roaring to go and swallow you up with
One bite –
Just make it across
When the teeth of the beast with its iron
Jaws burn its hot breath at my back.
I elope past the protective
Arch of Hadrian into the shadows of the
Cool alley along the Gardens that belong
To the Nation
Yet I still feel the Lion's heated breath
Even with my sped-up gait
Rush towards the hill
Past the Kallimarmore Stadiou
That keeps all the beauties waiting
Ahh!
At least this uphill task below the

Sweet-scented colonnade of acacia trees
That form a bower of shaded space with
Cooled air
The rising sun has not yet matured in its
Stripping powers f late morning's heat.

Then I peak on the apex near noble men's
Resting place
And my eagerness for life is great.
Still I have slowed down to half speed
Myself
I'm feeling afraid of getting on with age.
I love her.
I feel drawn to her arms
Her lips
Her eyes
Her thighs enclose me like a magnet.
I want to be with her
But I know she isn't well
And I'll never push her
But will I be palpably close to
Touch her?
It's at least a chance
And in between the chores she heaps
Her love upon her only child
She kisses me
Free and unbridled
With as much love as ever.
I do get hard.
I want her.
I feel happy to be with her
Without any fear
Any bad conscious
I feel I live since many years with

This extraordinary woman
Her body that responds to mine
This mind that wants to fuse with
Mine soon again.
My hand in her pants
I feel her flesh I desire
The shape of her spine and the
Bow of her arching
The fullness of her breasts
I do not rip-out yet from their
Soft-held bra
But let my hands slide over her and
Feel her body across
Stroke and shape it to my taste.
I kiss her deeply and she responds
To my desires to want her.
We want, how happy, how radiant
We are again!
I'm hard and she touches my penis
Through my pants
The moment her child rings
The doorbell.
She is rather sweet and blessed
With innocence
An artistic talent
The same way stubborn as she was
And as blood is thicker than water
Almost to the point
That we could be in bed altogether
Sampling the lust from one generation
To another
A never-ending chain of love that'll
Carry on forever...
Will it forever?

Nightfall and I read her message -
In love that is to a friend, collocutor,
Co-author, lover, son and brother:
Thank you Z for staying with me
For so long this morning –
I hope you are well tonight,
I'm happy you are here...

Well then I do reply:
I caress your body's writing pose
Kiss your heart that beats deep in me
Inspiration opens wide like your
Well-shaped thighs...
Compelling to my lips
My throbbing cock turned pen
That slides with love words
Upon this notebook of your soul.
ZZ.

There the moments to sit close
Together
Change to the desire
That is tenderness and gentleness
In midst f my hands sliding on her thighs
With my desires that pervade her
Like the warming air outside
That penetrates with pregnant hot
Sweetness this air inside around us
Where we sit together in our mind's
Nakedness and caress our beings
Together
Underline our want with palms that
Rub along our skins

Your fingers that touch my chest
Firing-up my nipples
That stick through my soft top
Like knobs you play upon
The door to my erotic entry into
This world we have created
Since many sequential years.

I wanted you to touch me
Slide upon me and let me heal
In your body's nearness
Give myself to you to wake in a
Demanding pose
Penetrating your giving body
To be mine.
Then as we touch more and grope
And taste this love that never had
A beginning
Nor will it ever have an end
Or so I believe.
I LIVE AND BREATHE.

3
THE THIRD DAY (Tuesday)

The night was interrupted
Aches and pains of B woke me
I made her tea and when consoled
Her
Cared for her reflux of acidity that
Could kill her
Made her sit-up in bed and wait for

Her calming tea
Then she reclines into bed again.
I then enter some notes about my
Feelings toward Ana, while Aleta sleeps
And Anetha dreams about her
Cunnilingus
And I close my eyes to imagine her
Face, her recent face I have held between
The palms of my hands for that velvet
Touch and the smooth desirable shapes
She lets my fingers run over
As if my love would wash across her sighs
As she's in a sudden move
Bent forward
While my hand drives deeply into the
Back of her pants.
I feel the soft roundness of her bums
The articulate channel of her spine
That ends in her vee-cut above her fold
How beautiful she's kept
Sensuously still awake.

I walk uphill with easy strides
Reach the apex of this road
That reminds me of Moussaka
And a cozy tavern
I wish to be with her – alone.
It is time to go and get the rest of
My downhill walk behind me.
A man who picks his nails sits
Opposite on a bench from me
Lacking lean clothes and love.
Would he be here if someone
Cared with kisses and even with

A slight compassion?
Would I be here if I did not care
Not care for her with a deep-seated
Love
And then hold her and give her
My total human dedication
Like everything to give in love?
Then I come towards her door
It's a bit slower by me, my approach
And by her to hold open her door.
Still we feel being drawn together
Even if she has grown now slight
Different views on life
Something that touches me deep
Perhaps there's joy I give her and
Enough excitement that she can
Reach her height
My hands on her all the time
I cannot keep off her and in her
Illness she has identified with a
Healing process and the team of
Administering good spirits
Who gather to save her life that
Medically seen still has gaps
Only love could bridge her pain.

I stand in the shadows of a love
That has turned its face to the wall
And now will have to live from touches
Less fiery excitement
And the doubts that come and go
Like rays of a critical path that oscillates
To laws love plays in a different way
Almost as s diminutive part in her life.

But I tend to think differently
Indeed.
There's so much besides the scientific
World
That can only be healed with unshakable
Love - And being of a stealthy act
Judged quickly as a despicable act
By those that are closest to your
Soul.
With these worlds I wrestle as much
As you do
Besides some strange sickness
That had befallen me
And I do not know if it's not just in
The mind
That causes me to suffer along
And share your self-punishment
As you say
Although that is not the case at all
But perhaps with me it is
As if something has turned and
Twisted me around
With such incredible force
Wedged in between your feelings
And mine
A break that pushes our emotions
Aside
But it fails doing it with success.
It never could win
Only burst into a spray of cold sparling
Fires that fall onto my body to raise a
Rock
That has evolved as a basis upon which
Nobody else can dwell or walk about

But the creation of our merging souls.
And while I lie in bed and dream of your
Naked presence
That I need besides what we call
Carezza
Is the nearness and the warmth I feel lost
Without and fade away
Losing my zest for life so easily
I could not believe that I could.
I write you some lines of a poem of mine
Onto the first page of the brown notebook
I gave to you
Something you like
But more – something you will know as
The truth.
I was told by a fellow writer that there's
No place in literature for the untrue.

Then you call me to your chair -
That does recline and where you rest -
To kiss you and I do
Just waited for you to be ready for me
To take me to your heart again
Like the standing act before
That's though wanted
Still tainted with guilt
Perhaps more from your side than from
Mine.
I touch you and grope you
Slide my finger into you...
And then onto you and back again
Make your body sing
Kiss your clit and watch it rise
Slide upon it

Rub it into your cum…
You need much more than as I do
Mine.
That is more difficult to achieve
Under these tightly restricted rules
You feel yourself subjected under.
But I can wait for my joy that is
Fulfillment of yours first and sometimes
I will be ready to burst and then at
Another time you can share the joys
Of good sex.
For now I want to touch you
Love you, kiss you, and lick you
Until you feel like a woman yet again
Risen from the underground of fright
And pain
Walking-up the long path of testing
Times to the world of our rock
We have created together again.
I am hard for a long time
Longest time ever from our petting
Today.
But then, as I have suddenly to leave you
I realize a terrible void that frightens me
To bits and I feel thirsty, swollen-lipped
And the words come with difficulty
From those lips that feel strange.
I start to stammer and walk to a place
We have met for the first time a few
Years back
But it has hanged
Like everything changes
Besides I was thinking about my love
To you

And how it would be to stay alive
In this new world of inner turmoil
We have compassion to overcome
Love with its many shades to come.

You may sit in your recliner and
Listen to your music I do miss.
There's lots of stillness around me
Without you, my love,
My continuous inspiration.
Then this dialogue comes clearly to
My mind...yes it is about reinstating
Of our love
Something we had lost for a while
And now we have found afresh, alive
And still pulsating,
Reaching out and getting close to
Each other we have shared our juices
Of life
In such exciting melting in my arms
With a probing finger
I've tasted you so fine
I can smell your hair, your skin, and
Taste your lips from caressing and kissing
And I love your touches that stir me
Make me grow hard.
I'll give you my love and all my feelings
I have for you, all combined into this
Physical belonging.
You are in my arms and in my hands
I fell asleep, had a dream and then
I woke to recall its frightening contents
I could see that I wasn't satisfied
Wishing to lie on a bed with you and just

Have once a peaceful Love-in
A carezza I picked up notions of
Forever sweet togetherness
Which you told me is impossible and
I should know that
But I don't want to know.

Why do I feel fallen-out of the sky?
I hope I still could give you the happiness
That you need to heal!
And now I'm dreaming, half-awake
And perhaps somewhat distanced from
Hard reality.
I still hang-on to purest feelings
Even if they appear egotistical to others.
Your words come back now as if we may
Never stop talking
Never will stop caressing with these
Strokes that are sensuous from your hands
Delicious kisses from your lips on me.
I wish we may continue our love talk
Our body talk-togetherness
To crown our merging minds.

4
THE FOURTH DAY (Wednesday)

Then in the heat of the afternoon
I slid into bed and slept
Although I wanted to write some more
Like in loving Aleta
I wished to stroke her more
But a climax will not come to me

Perhaps I am impatient and I need
To write my fill at first and reach
The gates of such a goal
I have set myself and then allow
Myself to peak as a prize
A treat
Or these moments of love we once
Shared and physically had
Are now something of the past
We'll treasure in the mind.
If love and excitement are emerging
In their source from the mind
Then if illness as such will be
Conscious in the mind
Then it could be switched-off
By such mind
Starved-out and dried up
As often love's fate is dealt with
Quite this way.
However, love then could mutate
Impossible to stop or be told:
It's enough!
It will never be stopped and
Carries-on regardless of conscious
Thought and tries for control
Which ends up in love's playful lap
Wayward child of Aphrodite
With his careless smile.
Then what are we humans in the
End?
The colourful flotsam that will by
Mere incident be swept onto the
Soft sanded beach.
And if we lie next to each other

We are blessed with good luck
For we have found this way of being
Together in the endless universe.
This morning bright and cool
Has now signaled the way and
Matters will be carried forward
And I do not foresee a future here
If you have left and travel to other
Shores
And you cannot tell me whereto
As we are on this blue planet
Merely visitors without a known
Itinerary but only to the gods
That have since ancient times
Abandoned us as it was their time
That had come-up
Which we still marvel about
Built sciences around.
And now as we feel compassion
Toward each other
We stare together at night -
Each of us alone – at the stars
And while I think about your love
And observe the waxing of the moon
Almost full soon
I feel my time has come to merge
This time with you
To take the full extent
Not just a bit here and an indication
There
But then I'm afraid to hurt your inside
As if I'd toss into your heart a knife.

But then as I float on air in my

Lacoste-blue shoes
Along the cobbled pavements of
Lysistratous Street
The marbled walkways along
Amalias
Ad emerging from the shades into the
The June-lit morning's fresh air.
Across the double carriage roads
Blowing a mental kiss to Melina's
Frozen smile forever in the white
Shaped unfinished marble
 With just enough speed to reach
The safe and peaceful ground
And feel one foot already touching
Paradisiacal lands
Where poets are recognized and
Like trees cared for
Looked after for future generations.

The avenue now disturbed by the
Preparatory works for the games
That started at Olympia once
Thirteen hundred years now back
While the time-span I muse about
Is almost impossible to fathom and
To re-experience in total
Perhaps some pictures and depictions
That have stuck to the mind from
History lessons or
From the exhibition's artefacts
I still, piece by piece and repetitively
Absorb all the time
As I arrive at the gateway of the city's
East

The centre of the world with the only
Siege in mind of conquering the arts
And the heart of a woman I love
Since I was a child.
But then I had to leave and flee fiendish
Destructors of all kind.
And how hard it was really to come back
On a long and tedious road
That crossed a continent and Seven Seas
My personal ongoing travels
Maybe an Odyssey
Perhaps an Odysseus
Ulysses of modern times who
Emerged in post-modern aegis
With molecular transformations
Those who are merging with a love
On a similar wavelength
Those who are truthful, intense,
And having merged over the years
So many times
That we all lost count
Are reborn each time we'll meet
Every time we are striving thro'
Our ordinary lives
To be together anyway we possibly
Can. At any place, especially when we wish
To kiss and touch and make love, now,
At any moment if we could find the place
Of our natural nakedness
That is covered by convention and
The stealthy life
Projected to the outside
To leave ordinary lives around us
Enter the layers below and above them

In order to duck and dive as long as we
Have to protect this UNUSUAL LOVE
We have created along all our physically
Active lives.
I have now entered the underworld of
Love
Below a mountain of heaped-up
Conventional shards
Of outdated conventions
We have the guts and strength to
Sideline to the importance of desire
And physical lust
Almost unbearable and riddled with
Sexual hangovers
That are worth every fuck in the world
With someone you love. INDEED!

Meanwhile I have overcome the dark
Shades of hurdles to get to my love
And see her right again, slowly, steadily
Ad repetitively, almost fanatically
Intending to love her
Increasing her libido step by step ad flow
By flow-
She'll taste sweet and spicy right now
Love without an end
However we suppress the final act
However we stop the immediate screw
The tremendous heavenly lovemaking
We'll do all these touches, gestures,
Eye-to-eye close-ups, lips to lips, grazing
Faces, limbs and bodies, skins and hearts
Minds and souls.

This morn' of all the morn's before
When I was deeply aroused
You have become aroused just by my
Being around and as I stroked you
Like a cat, a soft and sympathetic feline
A good and gentle eyed canine.
When, as we mix our chemistry with our
Touches I the abandonment of guilt
That has been fostered into us by the
Traditional rites
We love with our eyes and our close-up
Beings
And you show signs of waking-up
Being aroused today
Like I have been yesterday
And then you shine, smile, and I feel
Like shining, smile myself as well.
I have been transferred into you
Like you have transmitted yourself
Deeply into me
Oh how I do live and thrive with you
So close and next to me
And I cannot touch you now as I wish
Cannot take your pants off here
In the midst of Syntagma Square
And let you sit upon me in harsh
Daylight and screw the wits out of me.
Let us go into a spin to match the
Orbit ad get-off together
Spirited high and higher ad burst
Like Greek Fire.
I wonder what would happen
Could people see us?
Or would they pretend to be blind?

5
THE FIFTH DAY OF MEETING
(Thursday)

There – I wonder about my dreams
That pull me up and let me fall and
Rivers flow and cut between lives and
Sudden death -
The flow of this creative process lies
Between the living and the transitory
Space
That calls upon us like the extent of sea
And sky nobody scaled yet
Nobody succeeded entirely
Nobody can
But dreams can muster everything.
As the crack f dawn shimmers upon
The eastern horizon casting deep
Shadows between the columns f the
White-knighted Parthenon
Rendering the hills in blackened green
And profiling the pointed pines as lances
Of the worriers that march below the
Sacred Rock
In blushing taints of an awakening bride
I rise my eyes to scale the disc of the moon
That sinks into the arms of the sun's
Rising youth.

Light of the world will switch-on
In a steady unstoppable flow and
My mind becomes alert to the warble
Of birds, the bulbul's cries and the
Shrike's trill, the moosebird's crackles

But those are still in my dreams
But here the whining of cats in heat
And the dogs who chase with barking
Enticement
Before all falls still for a while
And the noises of an awakening city
Starts their murmuring machines
Into the new day of their woes and
Joys
The loves and cries in the revolving
City's sighs we all take a tiny part
Even our deep concerns for a love that
Glows in the dark like the brightly
Painted moon
That subsides between the pines
On the foot of the city' Acropolis
The repeating sighs and breathing
Of the land that enters this sixth day
Of being in a state of an asphyxiating
Love
Lying in a bed of desire and yearning
That has transformed into some love
Of being here for each other and feel
Compassion
Yet stirred erotically now and then
Unexpectedly in midst of a play of
Eternal tides.

This morning might be though different
To all other ones
As life and loving always will be
Even the way I rise and face the new day
The new challenge to be
Just to exist and project myself to my new

Extended boundaries
I have come across for days by which to
Enter circles that are built anew
As the love has t scale new mountains
Scout new ways to reach the apex
And perhaps find a way to cope
Besides topping the newly built bridges
Of emotion ad share the feelings, the
Moment that is given by means of an
Inner peace
By means of togetherness we seek
Continually since we were born
Yet only for me it meant to wait for
You another seven years.
But then I had not yet experienced
Love in a harmonious unison with a
Woman of a sensual response
As I have with you for so many times
So many times we were together in
This burning love
That took its toll of burning out inside
Of us.

Now, how on this fifth time to see you
What do I expect?
To love you to the utmost and to push-off
All barriers of desire
That have since day one enflamed in us
Like hell.
In this expectation of the utmost
It's possible that I get ill
Ill with a fever I cannot explain
Ill with the boils of love that shout-out
From my body like the blisters of a

Tormenting burn.
Have I been punished for these deeds
Of fornication with an inexplicable cough
A haunting trepidation that gathers acidity
In my loins?
Is this the day of reckoning that has
Arrived?
That will drive the steel wedge into our
Hearts to separate us forever
By bleeding to love's death?

I do then wonder why?

And into the mid-morning's lay
Our bodies are placed tightly together
First, I do love you in a way
I have not made to any plans
Nor have I wished I would
Just fantasized and wanted you
Maybe I wanted you so much
I was excited all the previous day
And with your presence I got aroused
Much more and more as we touched
And fused
The moment of our first screw
The build-up to the perfect first
Initiated crown-to-clit-touch
The touch I dreamed of, that I might
Not ever have so quickly
Well, so soon, it was as if I was again
In the lustful land f Ana, Aleta, Anetha
And they all wanted me and I promised
To be just that: Their Man. Her man,
Who sits naked on the bentwood-chair

In a trance of her heavenly screw
As she smiles and pens her lips
Darts her tongue and throws back
Her head
Moving up and down on my pride
Of an erected penis
That she allows sinking into her
Like a fitting sword into its well-oiled
Sheath and then again to pull it out
She moves fast and rests at times
Between sweet penetrating want and
Deep and deeper sighs of noisy
Breathing
Like excitements press from her
Breasts when she rides me in her
Growing lust and I did not expect such
A deep-seated screw with a lustful
Twist and turn a turn of her height
That nears now soon –
I want her to cum without reserve
Just come and cum and cry and never
End
Just one more time and then again.
How Do I enjoy her lustful ride
I close my eyes and let her do me and
I say: Aleta, you screw so well and fine
And I feel purest lust…I never want to
Cum now fast and I twist the nipples f
Her gorgeous breasts
Take them into my mouth one by one
To suck her like a kid his mother
Greedy for her milk that runs now deeper
Still and even more
And even wetter I wish to stay in her

Womb
That cuddles my crown between her soft
And large pink discs
And suck her into another height
I do. I never stop until she gasps and sighs
Reading her climactic signs
She always closes her eyes and throws
Her head back when she comes.

How beautiful is love as I ask her
To turn and let me screw Ana one more
Time and sweeten my thrusts –
I can move lying supine – into her
Holding her bums and pushing into her
Movement's shadow of Anetha
Who watches from the door
And like a ghost approaches
Touching me with a kiss.
Now I may reach nay height much more
Easy
More concentrated with deeper want
As I top her cum with mine
Just now I see the faces of three women
I love and well in lust covered from all sides
In this cluster of love that roars me to a
Final height.
I cry-out, muffled as I bite into her arm
She stretches me backward with
Her other one playing my balls. Now!
Spray now and once more!
I loose count this morn'
This rapid rising morn' of our stars
Crossing of constellations with our limbs
In lustful embraces

Tender movements
Of a first-seated fuck that enticed me to
Stand up and let you bend down
Move into you in piston-slides
Into your pussy hard and soft and hard...
Your hands hold fast the spiral frame
Of your marital bed
And I hear some squeaks and sighs
Alternating
When I get wild in my cum and
You move of me fast:
That is too much!
Ah it's so much fire.
Such burn!
And I have sunken back into my seat
Mouth-gaping , knees jellied, softened
Collapsing on your bentwood chair I love
I loved before
But now it's unusual
Pure lust as it always was in me and
Will remain so here.
I love this fuck with you again
Arrived in AZZA-Land at last!

Then we all are though actors in this
Play of unusual relations
But lucky we have to give-up nothing
Not a thing , not any relationship
A need, a conclusion
A conclusion that is strange rather
Than weird.
I think I am pissed – the poet writes.
There are matters of passion
Fervour you cannot control.

Even now I have to what I have written:
OH GOD I'LL DIE IN THE BATHTUB,
IN THE SHOWER, IN CAFÉ'S, IN THE
PLACES I'VE ALWAYS MET YOU.
Do we think we'll die together in lust
And love?
ARE WE?
Yes we are continuously so
Immediately we touch and desire
Invades our veins like an infection,
INDEED!

6
THE SIXTH DAY (Friday)

What an early morning for a hangover
Too much ouzo - I guess – in between
Musings about despondency
To sit and wait
Being unable to help
Feeling sorry for oneself?
Probably.
Probably, who knows?
I got-up early to write a few lines for
Ana, for Aleta, for Anetha
And I found out that I got nearly
My knickers in a knot
Just like Alexander the Great
Who did seek eternal life
Find the source to be sanctified...
Athens, city of poets, writers, artists
Inspiration everywhere
At least almost preempts that point

And touches one's mind.

The Giza pyramids, the Chinese wall
Enigmas that don't stir us as much
As it did everyone last century.
Now I prepare to see you
See you as a friend, a lover, someone
Who is your healer, not your conscious
But your good spirit, your good ghost
Your friend, your ardent lover who has
Only one demand:
THAT YOU GET WELL!
This is a cultural revolution
Something that's in us and it will have
To be carried around with us like
A stone
A gemstone that is precious to the
Moment, set-into our minds and the
Claws of our imaginations.
I love the moment of getting-up
With a positive mind
Seeing you and the whole cahoots
The spread-out wings
The fanning thighs
And the opening of the lips that
Emit the sighs that make me rise
To the occasion.
Even if we cannot lie in bed together
Our needs have to be satisfied with
The touches on the outside –
We love , we touch each other at
Odd times
And in between at peaceful times
That are challenged by the desires

Of our innermost
And we have just a few minutes for
A deep kiss, the touch we seek thro'
Tight jeans and clothes that are soft
Yet like second skin.

Reclining into her dark and ship-like
Hull of an automated existence
I join her at times of a relative
Conscious mind
With swift caresses
The low-tide that keeps us close
Together for some intimacy
Most important to keep our love
That's handicapped by a stealthy
Character
But perhaps due to its secrecy it's
Kept vivid, emotionally hopeful
And alive
Until we meet like a star-crossed
Loving pair that's free
For having a tightly entwined
Heavenly relationship
A joyous ride of real fornication
That's sweet and out of this world
At all times.
As your strength has faded
Left you suddenly pale and
Bloodless
As I observe you sitting next
To you
In a closeness still saved by the
Comfort of your seat we'll use
This opportunity to unlock your

Stationary car and let our bodies
Drop inside as if it were a waiting
Room
For you to see your medical doc
Who knows of some poison that
Could stop the growth of a virulent
Snake that eats you up inside
Stop its destructive life
For at least some time and sets
You up onto this road of a bearable
Life again
We have still left time to stride
Onto hills and undulations of
This city of marble shards
That has for many thousand years
Emerged in a see-saw life of
Growth and savage death and
Thought about as the best ever
Built, sacked and rebuilt, and
Sacked and built up yet again
For even greater admiration
On the layers of ruins that are
Planed and excavated scientifically
Where we all looking for our
Connection to the past
Our chains of love that had
Carried on our existence
As I do look upon you for my
Being, my guidance to this
Present layer
We do move and slide upon
Together
Or just rest and touch our
Aesthetically pleasing excitements

Adorned by the rising tides from
The sea of lust and high above
White gulls swerve and circle with
Their mates in a swift and sailing
Mode that is my touch upon you
My gentle merging strokes to your
Heart
Until it penetrates your soul
In a lustful soar in the warming air
Of June –
Above the Sacred Rock we fly.

There, I did not know I would be
In a groove of love that'll extend
Itself day by day then morn' by morn'
Into the pallid-blue sky of June of
Another Athen's day. Indeed.
I rushed towards the emerald hill
The apex of a dream that followed
Me day by day and night by night
Almost entirely mesmerized I was
Will be with you at all times. I will.
I know now
It also too late to have a change of
Hearts
Besides, the moods that dictate
These words
Let me guess ad project a mood
That I often abandon at the first step
Into your domain
Passed the threshold down the two
Marble steps that mean the world to me
Indeed a world that I have come to appreciate
And learned to value

Bit by bit as it appeared not only in my dreams
But also in my creative work
My living style, my breathing, my healing,
My wellbeing, my all:
My A, my Ana, my Aleta, my Anetha, my
Alpha to Omega –
This is the Attic smile
The kiss of a dusky-eyed woman
That made me come alive
Every time we meet and press our
Physical beings together
Fittingly and tight
Hand in glove
Head into thigh
Cock into cunt, alive, well, what final
Relief, shit!
I say: Why can't we do it all the time?
What's wrong?
Yu answer: Nothing's wrong.
Perhaps society is.

I love everybody A'a loves
And there's no point in denying that
Sexual love exists just between us now.
I would not mind B to have longings
Toward N, or L has for me perhaps.
Whatever.
I guess it gets as good as it does
Nobody will question:
Come Sunday
Nobody will question the erotic content
Of our songs in conversation much later
Do they?
I guess that B goes mad about me

Being away
Going to the museum like to church
Wandering to the library of the world
That'll combine our efforts
Writing love
Untouched and never discovered
Almost a victory unseen in modern
Times! Alas!
However, I do not care much about
Conventions
And cannot find sympathy with timid
Souls or people who pretend to be
Just different
But never really try
Too much afraid of being
Caught-out!

That's like B
She's curious if I lie naked on the
Sun-flooded terrace in front of the
Acropolis-view
Indecent exposure
Although I care not to offend
But in the end I don't worry at all.
I do not mind some people watching
Getting a high on my body's sleek
Lines, get-off on me
As I would get-off at times on them
If they are pretty.
We are all human and loaded with
The emotional ballast of our previous
Generations through sucking-up
Mother's milk.
I suck A's and it's perhaps not the

Sweetest milk per se
But It's like tasting my mother's milk
Sweet and with a sense of discovering
Lascivious well-being
Like with A
But then I'm here on a Friday
Bent forward with lust and desire
More in a way of scaling the barriers
And do not know how I will feel
Caressing her
Hugging her into the world
She calls AZZA
That's a state of being
The sunshine that penetrates my skin
Sitting in the corner of this terrace
In the corner of the world
That beats outside to a rhythmical
Tune
Kept alive by the local beat
That wants us erect and aroused all
The time
To spend the dollar and dime on their
Delicate economy
But also I do not yield as an artist to all
This titillation of commerce and in the
Name of sport and then all's done there
There's still mythology.

I come to you in lithe strides
Of a young and unbridled semi-god
Sprung from the nymphs and satyrs
From the caves of the bases
Into the Sacred Rock
Which gape like open wounds

Like a pussy that opened-up
To welcome this desirous move of
My cock
That has never been up so much
To never-tiring demands of your
Mind and soul
And the desirous dive into a deep
Deep void in my entire life
A void caused
By my mother's death
Her change from a loving being
To a Medusa's heart
The snake turning her poisoned
Heads toward my restricted breath.
I do inhale you
Mother of my fantasy
Lover of my heated loins
In a well-perfected love
That I am seeking at all times
I do not know when to get enough
Of
Like a bear that gorges himself on
Honey and steppe grass
And rodents and salmon
Drunk with desire of love
In their imminent spurn-jumping
Right into the lazy bear's pointed
Fangs and their open mouths
To cum in their lustful bitten
Death?

And this is a time of not complete
Swallowing of arousals and erections
Yet it's as I do take her perturbed

Sweetness that's temporarily not
In tune with sexual desires and this
Is all right with our free-love believes
And the ways we devour each other
For now we want sexual relief
Besides the enjoyments of climatic
Highs – of course this is the life we need
The life we wish to have every day
We will. Just for now we'll have.
And B says: I love to eat and enjoy my
Food almost lasciviously –
Just as I enjoy A now
And always did in a lewd and gentle way
That is inimitably sensuous and I go mad
Bumping her bums and push and pull
And get her to her height and a cry
Then just lie there being screwed by her
Until my welling lustful fuck will take
Over
And I turn her bums and push into her
Wetland deep and wildly
Until I cum.

This is not a town I wish to slip loose
Like a stone that rolls along dislodged
To vanish out of sight
Hitting against other stones
Until smashing into town's centre
NO.
I NEVER WANT TO.
Especially I know the smile of two girls
I like right now.
One is older and a forerunner of the
Younger one

You could say she is part-daughter of
Her mother
As I am the son of her mother
Making us sister and brother.
Indeed, this is the desired incest of
My most intimate dreams
A perfect lover and Ana's offspring
Well, only the ONE
But then it might be just the thing
To do.
She's got a great mind
One that one day will meet mine
She said and for the moment I see
Ana's face that is mine alone
But is it now?
I'm not sure in my mind any more.

7
THE SEVENTH DAY (Saturday)

And all was done on the seventh day
Perhaps the food was bought
The roses lay almost spent
In the tentacles of the late afternoon.
In its own heat the city cooked
Its tin-boxed meat and the birds did
Fly as usual upon the granite rock
Circling to the whirls that came from
Deep inside the Sacred Rock
And all was done on the seventh day?
Almost.
There are some presents
And some leopard spots

There are outlines of elephants
Lined-up to be feasted upon
Like on the rocks of the caves and
Ravines
We were roaming about
Not so very long ago!
WE HAVE NOT MUCH TIME
She would say to me
And I had all the time in the world.
I did not understand.
There was music and some more
To see and to write about
And I guess I should have brought
Along another blank notebook for
Aspiring writers
To write.
And all was done on the seventh day
Though there were laughs and
Good friendship
Such a great and thriving company
And then there was the river of an
Undercurrent of love
Flowing through the bodies that were
Coming and going and touching
And I was close to her
Close and wanting to be closer yet
As if we were accepted as a pair
Of roses in the vase of a Monet's
Orange glow.
Then it rained words ad anecdotes
And some exquisite smart search
To uncover some spots of your youth
And a faint desire of holding hands
And be involved like the doves on the

Newly marbled Square
The hands that cannot rest
Sprout like bamboo
Rushing to grow thru' everywhere.

This must be the night
When the covers fell like petals to the
Floor we caress on
Steady at first and gentle
And I give names, letters of the alphabet
To the players
Alpha and Omega
The hot and fornicating pair
And N and L, Beta and Lambda
And then back to Alpha and Beta
Falling-in ad lined-up in a chain that
Moves along and around a table in a
Snake-dance
Into the room and out the window
Drawn back by libidinous draughts
Into her main domain
And then slipping into the smart
Laptop of Alpha's computer
Swallowed-up and captured in its vaults
Of data to come alive
When Alpha will press the retry-button.
Am I a slave of buttons and of the laptop's
Lewdness?
And even if, what is the sense of thinking
In negative terms?
Jealousy and a life that has slipped out
Of one's hands?

NO! There is the daily touch

The daily close and fast togetherness
At all times
Will not be anything else
For me the miracle of love
For the mind a continuous inspiration.
The poet has still lewd thoughts and love
Is hidden everywhere
He smiles.
The soft-lit atmosphere conducing to his
Thoughts
Of mingling bodies and this orgy of
Interaction in social intercourse.

Outside the noises grow louder from
People neglected in their simple worlds
Of lacking recognition for just being
Lack of even existing
Bleating of stirred-up sheep
TAM TAM TAM...
In rhythmic beats
That recall boots marching
Armies
The invasion of Barbarians...

And she comes close to me
Sensing her opportunity to fix the silver
Bangle on my right wrist her way
Close to me and she does all right
Then tells me about her mind and
Mine
That have touched
Perhaps will meet in the near future
For togetherness – perhaps!
But then she feels challenged

Competing for a slice of this poet's
Love
Who remains in the wings and
Watches us like her most-beloved
Children – son and daughter
Competing for laurels
Competing for her motherly love?
In this friendly competition I write
Instant poetry and verses that are
Spontaneous
Yet not continuing for long
As Lambda is all over the place
Pacing up and down the confines
Of her lounge
In a hectic mode
Forgetting about the love that a poet
Might have toward his poetess
She'll sense it but cannot fathom
All there is confined to his innermost
She cannot be in the know of tragedy
And the pain she's ignorant of
Kept in the dark of her sheltered
Childhood.
But she'll soar soon enough
To some artistic heights
If she' prepared to work quite hard
Maybe harder as she was used to.

And Sunday the poet is at rest.

BOOK II
DAYS 8 TO 16

8
THE EIGHTH DAY
(Monday)

There's a feeling of a void in
Our love
That is now in compassion-mode
Rather than in fulfillment of one's
Desires and one's needs
We have created together.
I take it as personal punishment
Not due to L being present
Not because N is her legal spouse
But her person incapacitated by
Her terminal ills
She reacts thus strangely.

I do not know where to go
Where to my steps will take me
In a foreseeable future
What to put onto paper
And how to find my slightest
Creative groove.
Fate has wedged L between us
The pretty one to pursue and the

Mind wishes to be with
Yet I don't know if we ever could
Be close together
Under such a weight of fate's
Circumstances
Could we?
There are times opportune to kiss
As she takes leave to attend to her
Studies
But then the atmosphere is not
Inductive for love. It cannot be.
Hardly any place to go now and
A is not prepared to make love
In her weakened state
After all I'm dislodged
Only if B would be in love with her
She would be interested in sexual
Relations much more
Perhaps she was in the past
Indicating it to me at two or three
Occasions - Gathering experience –
As she put it to me.
I'll need some human fleshly contact
I guess there's the subway to Piraeus
Or the bus 049?

The pet thinks his way and he knows
That he'll never do that yet
As that part of Z's life has been left
Behind in the dark and dangerous
Lands turned into recently.
He has no cough, no sinusitis, and
He'll enjoys the hard-ones he's
Getting after a snooze

Or a good night's sleep.
He does touch them and he'll take
It a bit further in the afternoon
When he had closed his eyes and
Felt as if A would touch him
The way she always did in the
Immediate past.
He still has vivid scenarios in front
Of his mind's eye
Her hands flicker through his skin
And her lips taste his swollen crown
When sweetness of a virtual kiss and
A real touch merge
He sighs
Suppressing a cry next to his dear
Spouse
Who sleeps
Pressing his finger-lock too late at
The base of his cock
And he spills some juices
Milky white...he comes:
AHH! A! Ahh! I LOVE YOU!
As if she'd then would sense his
Excitement
And reveal with him the way
SHE STILL CAN DO IT.

He'll sit with A who falls asleep
In her fav couch-chair. Reclined.
He'll sit on the couch she once
Loved him on
And he writes some stanzas
Into his red-black notebook she
Gave him as a present.

Recently
To fill its innocent pages with his
Devourment, fire, and ravishing
Notes, verses that burn it all to
Ashes.
He shows her his ELEGIES.
She considers as his lament.
Well, he says, perhaps in a way it
Had turned-out to be
This third time.
He does though avoid drifting into
Sadness too deeply
For her sake
Rather enjoy your sleep while I write!
He tells her
As if his wish and hers would gel
Instantly
Even under such unfortunate signs
Of ill breezes and stormy unsettling
Times.

Together they feel bonded and she
Falls asleep...
Well, as if she'd be near his chest.
Her sounds of breathing close at his
Ears, even as if she'd turned on the
Volume
As if she'd lie intimately on top of him
All the time
Just as she always wished it...
Close and near.

What goes on in his life now?
Well, what will go on in a lover

Who has not recognized deep in his
Heart the need to combat these
Shadows of death in a courageous
Head-on fight?
He'll fight and he'll fight tough
He could be exceptionally
Hard-assed
To get through this PAIN.

9
THE NINETH DAY
(Tuesday)

And the poet writes:
He'll wake again with rigor and
Filled in his heart with growing
Expectations
That'll give him strength
For walking the stretched-out
Gardens
The hill that takes him up into the
Townships which have such great
History attached
As he read in the various cultural
Museums and the way the Greek
Do think and act in general
Some like Ephialtis always will exist.
He is glad to walk and further his love
To bring upon her
To soar like a seagull from the vicinity
Of the gulf and glide with the upwind
Stream across the Acropolis and slide

Along in free fall upon this cushion's
Flow
Deliver her a letter of his love in the
Beak of a dove
White dove of his heart
And spend love on her that'll heal her
Additionally
Speed-up her wellbeing
Get her on her feet one again.
Or when he tucks her into bed to
Sleep with her Geek-Style
Any style
All styles she wishes
All to get her up again
Breathe into her life and raise her
Body
As he would a flailing balloon
To soar renewed.

She's quiet. Not well.
But they'll walk to the shops
And then in a moment's stress
Climb into her car
And sit side by side and touch a
Bit and let her recover.
He is concerned and he'll suffer
Quietly with her for a while.
Then he'll take her by her hand
And guide her along and slowly
Up to her place.
He'll have some coffee with her
And then he'll to her
Some of his recent verses.
Indeed she inspires him for his

Poetry
His work depends to a great extent
On her and the tenor of his select
Words
And on how she feels.

At moments of her reappearance
And physical awareness she'll kiss
His lips
Praising their fullness and their
Colour red.
Moments of tenderness
With hands holding and sliding
Sweet gentleness and his growing
Arousal that'll come and go
Like her sleepiness followed by
Her wake.
But even if he walks out the door
Into the hall
He's aware of her at all times
At every turn he feels her
As if she'd lived with him for
Many years.

And now he feels responsible
For her
And her state of being that has
Deteriorated from one day to the
Next
Overnight
As if some giant spook had squeezed
The lights of day from her senses
Rendering her a ghost herself.

His love turned into compassion
With immediacy of his appearance
Seeing her in her fading state f flushes
And restlessness.
How would he – at this heart-ripping
Moment – not show love t her?
And in spite of his disappointed state
Of being he still found ways in his
Innerness
To be with her, doing chores for her
And to keep a continued liaison of
Their hearts going
Beating below the stealthy surface of
Their momentary intimate lives
That have not floundered between the
Shards of antiquated sites or the grey
And blue painted blocks
Squeezed tightly together in a
Phalanx against imminent dangers
That face the often beleaguered city
The lands which were abused and
Sacked
As was the punishment for refusal
Of for subjugation
To a greater force of men and mean
Leaders.
And often enough there were calls:
Where are the Gods to help us now?
Since the many of thousand years
All these cries will lie like letters of
Dire pleas
Heaped upon the threshold of the
One and ONLY GOD?

But then s do lie the trillions of
Sparkling stars beside the abandoned
Souls of desperate, unhappy sighs
Condensed in the blanket river of the
MILKY WASTELAND
Nobody spends more time on
But a smile
Story-time telling for children and
The appearance for the appearance
For the curiosity of men
Visiting the recommended sites
Furthering the eco-tourists rise
Their armies of purely consumerist
Minds.

She'll fall asleep when the poet
Is around
And she'll broker in his desires
He cannot shower upon her
As she'll be too drowsy to respond
And be with him in continued unison
This is then as bad as his sickness in
Her
And it'll eat him-up entirely
Soon enough to leave the city without
A trace
Abandoned from the love of others
He does not even had a chance to meet
Yet properly
Though she does indicate to him some
Of her clan of women
Who had shown an interest in him.

10
THE TENTH DAY
(Wednesday)

She has a talent to turn-on and
Then turn-off anybody towards
Her likings or dislikes
As she showed to him photographs
Of her family and then as well
Someone she knew from Online
She adored perhaps
Someone from Northern lands
Another blonde
Not only in company of women
Just now
As she has to precede to town
The central hospital
To test her blood.
He feels his heart constrict at
Times and he wishes he could be
With her all the time
But then that's rather painful
Feels like being a martyr
An arrow that pierces him now
And then
And he cannot make love to her
That's why.

So he has compensational acts
Of autoeroticism and some
Re-direction of the forces in him

That'll take him to various places
Besides the museums:
Benaki. Jewish. He'll go to the
Acropolis any time.
But now it's the way to avoid
Self-destructive thoughts.

Will 'Starry Heights' provide the key
Or will it be the end of their affair?
The stealthy, non-existing bond
That is so strong and boisterous
He is afraid of falling victim of his
Heart to it?
Their being that's non-existing
Crying to be heard aloud by as
Many beloved as is possible
Right now.

He enters the marble hall
Of Benaki's and he is suddenly
Surrounded by the aura of beauty
And love
He feels aroused as he comes
Across this beautiful head
With soft-pursed lips in the
Half-open Archaic smile
He wants to kiss –
Pygmalion-like –
He touches the outline of
Her lips
And his heart beats fast.
Aphrodite. Aleta. Ana?
They all are one for him now
And he wishes her to stay alive!

And what will he give to save
Her? An arm and a leg?
Perhaps he has to walk across
The Attic lands and find her on
An island
Healed and in one piece again?
He'll give something up for her
But what'll it be?
Compassion is generally raised
To the surface
In all human beings
More in one
Less in another
He has turned his love
R most of it into.

Now that is what she wished and
Wanted
Although he is not sure if she'd
Still in a mental strength for that
To engineer
More so she has told him about
Many matters
Indicative of some future sketches
Her mind has suddenly released
To him
But then he's truthful
Trustworthy
And he could shape her into a
Protagonist
She'll like or perhaps dislikes
If he'll hit the nerve of truth in
Her

Opened-up its rawness with the
Scalpel of his pen
That had almost ceased to sense
The direction at the edge
Of his circle's fate
Had him cast about a city
That'll grow from shards and
Shavings of the learned and a cast
Of eternal drama, actors actresses
And a host of onlookers
That line the periphery of the
Theatre of the avenues, cafes, and
Well-trodden paths of the inner
City's magnetic body
That attracts these masses of
Moths
To its sweet-scented lit candles
Placed strategically
By mothers and by married
Women
Of deep and reverberating
Sensuality
The poet will react to
Pick-up on with his finely strung
Nerves
To match a tune to his latest song.
True, imaginative, sensuously
He'll point his limbs' extensions
To the parchment of the skins
He writes upon.

11
THE ELEVENTH DAY
(Thursday)

Each time another morning
Dawns
Rattling deeper into his
Conscious life
Rising monologues of reasoning
And doubts
Rendering his physical life with
The strain of lacking sleep
Causing nightmarish dreams.
He's looking up towards the
'Sacred Rock'
That had echoed in his mind
With the blasts of
Firework scenes
In orange, white, and blue
That coloured the granite stone
And inflamed the pure-white
Glowing marble that sang to him
In renewals of a lament.

And still he has not finalized
All questions he wished to ask
Her
All touches he did seek to give
To her
However well or troubled she'll
Indicate her body to receive them

And if she writhes with expressions
Of pain
That pierce his entire heart.
There's no space left any longer
To hide his feelings
Hide behind an appearance of a
God that proceeds with a cover of
Clouds around him
That has a power of absorbing all
Her loves
The way she would present them
To him
Stopping his own love for her
In its stealthy tracks.
But how could he now disguise
It all?
How can he love her now
Without some showing of true
Compassion
She has requested from him
Spending her tears before?
The day she told him her ordeal
The day the penny dropped
And while he wished to love her
She withdrew
Accusing him of a selfish act?
How could he now love
How could he?

Then into his own struggle
To come to terms with a changed
Life, a different view, and some drama
To follow
She'll pull-out an arrow and she rides

Her speeding horse across the
Silver screen of her life
Then he'll feel her pain much later
Once he'd become aware of the
Gaping wound and the scent of
Bleeding flesh he stares at
In his desire that toppled from her
Life as is
Turning its heavy weight onto him
One-sided he will fall from the
Lofty heights
A bird
That falls like a stone
Tumbling from above its flight
Across the Acropolis
That carries her temple
On its crystallized shoulders.

Will he be able to ever walk up
To her again?
Will he have the strength left
The will to follow his true desires?
Keep the blanket of a stealthy love
Drawn-up and extended beyond
His late and disappointed life
That lies now entirely open and
Bruised between the remaining
Marble shards
That'll seek a home among their
Brothers and sisters
Who sit already snug
And have moved into positions
Of clustered loves.

He writes his notes down in a
First and immediate burst
And then as she succumbs t sleep
He'll leave and he'll return
Then leave
To return again.
He does not know any longer
His future treat.
He'll retire from her like a dog
That has been given space to lie in
The sun
Sleep all day
Passing folk will never step upon
His comfortable lie.
He watches himself often
Musing about love and poetry
The moods that bring about his
Passion
That is suddenly abided and left
On the 'Sacred Rock'
In a cave
Shying away from daylight
Shying away from life.

There is though compassion
As requested from her
Enough to keep still going for
Another day or two
And now he has not touched again
The illness he had
The acid burn that electrified
Their only merging
Their only intimate piercing
Of their united souls

Since many months.
Now he has healed
But then she needs love and
Patience
HE HAS
But cannot give it openly to her
Without the wedges of a silver-cusping
Moon
Or the coming and going of Lia
The young and upcoming queen
And the sad squabbling of the Italian
Painter
The master of Mural Art and a friend
Of Saints and bearded Monks.

He'll take her chores and walk the
Liquefied streets
Until the soles of his feet burst into
Flames
And this punishment will drive him
Into the arms of a dead society of
Artists
T visual ad literary words
Into the coolness of the poet's
Waiting room
To heaven or to hell
He doesn't know yet
He wouldn't know the difference.

12
THE TWELTH DAY
(Friday)

This morning he'll take B for
A walk
See some of the great art
That one man had collected
All his life.
The rad is winding and far for B
Who struggles with life
Like with her walk.
The rising heat emanates from
Endless blocks of mortared bricks
And stone
Shutters closed on windows
Concrete and dark glass
And the flowing stream of tar
On which metal boxes
Like boats
Permanently float upon.

Here in the fashionable district
Close to the president's palace
There is a marbled space
Containing incredible beauty
Of the beginning of man's
Creative spirit in the arts
Forgotten are all the pains of
Walking
Standing on one's feet even

Longer still
Marvel at the artifacts
The emerging of Classical and
Hellenistic worlds
We feel close to
Hang our hearts on now for hours
Until we are famished
Having absorbed all the art we could
And our minds have touched upon:
Neolithic Man
Minoan Woman
Until the Hellenistic world
Stirred-up in us deep emotions
Human touches that went beyond
The general ad superficial
That will burn deep inside
Whenever I have strong and
Recurrent feelings to be with
You –
Be with Anna, Anetha, Aleta
Not in this particular order
But then you know how I am
And what I could be and would
Achieve.
WHAT?

I do not know I have chosen to
March forward and conquer
Feel great pleasure ad achieve
All I could
Besides, I can be the best friend
Yu ever had –
IN YOUR MATURE LIFE
A lover who still has unceasing fire

Glowing in his loins
And a collocutor for your life as a
Writer
Perhaps we both just feed from
Each other
Perhaps the relationship I dreamed
About
Is on the verge to happen
In such ways I still have dreams
About
And you are skeptical as usual
Analyzing
But I'll be more philosophical
About
While Lia will use the el3trical sparks
Of tension and write her stories
Be prolific
Thrive and ramble
Upon this ageing façade
Of a late neo-classical building
We have both dwelled-in
Many times
Made love
The way we always wanted to.
AND NOW?

13
The THIRTEENTH DAY
(Saturday)

Since late I feel drunk too
Much ouzo
The milky liquid
That brings my inner fire
To leaping ripeness
Leads me on to dreams
Of joy
I miss with you
The way we had.
I know I still hang on the days
Of golden lays
And silver-sliding passion
That had amalgamated in our
Bonfire of intensity –
Sweet
Intense and continual fusion
That traveled far beyond the
Blue Attic horizon
Of near-perfect days
Days in the stealthy state
Of FERVOUR.

Today I feel deserted and left
To seek the beach
That hosts other lonely people
Some lie close together
I do envy

As I lie apart from you
Asunder from my life
That so utterly changed
So different and colourless
Dried-out and milky-pallid
Like the late afternoon skies
That hover behind the great temple
And the temple sits still upon
The rock
And ain't sing today.

Neither do the birds
But their songs
Outgunned by the never-ending
Drumming
Of the bass guitar-humming
Traffic.
My eyes rest upon the young
And I feel young inside with the
Carapace of an aged man
Who is considered perhaps as a
Geezer at times
Perhaps I need the spirit of love
That has still to transform to the
Life I seek to have
After I'm gone...
This time though it'll break
My heart in two
This time I'll need all the strength
All hope I could muster
And even much much more
Than that.

And while we pass in a container

Of bodies and souls through the
Corridors of a congested life
I'll try to be with you
But then again I fail
But failing I ask why?
I never intend to fail you and
Not now
NEVER.
I need you and don't say so
I don't want to cause you
Emotional pain above all physical
Pains you have to grapple with
Besides.

Then there is your love extended
To me in images you feed my eyes
My mind with
And I have fallen in love many times
With you:
Asa kid
As a young woman
Have traveled the world to be with
You but always failed to reach you
Finally
Always had to choose secretly
Seeing you
And our emotional life had this
Stealthy over above it all.
A dampener to all our sounds
Of love
Consumed through earphones
And our suppressed emotions
Bubbling below our skins
In front of our respective families.

I look upon this young and svelte
Woman
Who inspires desire in any man
Even with the slightest of her
Movements of her perfectly-shaped
Body
Her coquette way of measuring-up
Anyone who looks at her with his
Secret wishes to lie with her
Glowing in his eyes.
There are others
All shapes and sizes
All over the beach
Lying like asleep
Perfectly blending in with the
Coloured pebbles
Some children play with on the
Edge of the polluted water.
We have an urge to leave it for the
Less-fussed persons
The rough and toughened-up.

The golden woman glows and she
Stops a man who excels in body
Paintings.
I try to understand her foreign
Language
She talks non-stop with her pure
Golden boy.
She has chosen a sword with a
Snake wound around a shaft
As an emblem to adorn her
Right shoulder

I wonder why?

When I walk together with B
Down some streets towards
A hotel we have missed last time
To get into
As it's too far removed from the
City centre
Where we chose to revel in night
Walks
Enjoying the magical atmosphere
Of city-reveling
The view of the lit-up ACROPOLIS
I could never get enough of
Like from the love I have with
YOU.

There' stillness and uneasiness
Without desperation
But with pain
That drips into my veins
Like an infusion
Day by day
As longer I stay
The more I feel it.
But then what do you feel?
WHAT PAIN DO YOU FEEL?
I hasten to abandon my personal
Feelings for a while
Until you feel better
Until you will be what you wish
To be
Until you live-up again to our
Dreams.

Then the pushing of bodies
In an overcrowded bus that
Came too late.
We have a hard time to get back
And finally have room to breathe
Have some drinks and go to bed
Wake again and get some supplies
Walk again between the candle-lit
Diners that add to the quaintness
With their murmuring patrons
Ad lovers with their cooing
We gaze across the water-clock
That's made of marble
Shaped as an octagon.
Finally a quiet walk through some
Abandoned roads and places
Emptying quite fast.
The city though is still alive.

I'm in her city
Visiting the place we have been
Together
Worked-up a stirring of deep-seated
Memories.

14
THE FOURTEENTH DAY
(Sunday)

There!
You've heard my calls
Came to rest with me in a dream
All these years of wandering
Through our young and growing
Lives
We have seen each other from
A distance
Touching in our minds
Too shy to come close physically
Well maybe not shy but not yet
Adjusted well enough with our
Senses that were rebellious to our
Physical unison
That has been born in our minds
The moment of our friendly kisses
When you came into my room
Where I sat close to your mother
Sister, spouse, and lover
And I spelled-out your name on
A piece of paper
I carry at all times in the pocket of
My pants.

I say aloud inside me:
Lee, Luise, Lou-lou ; Liah, you
Are my next sweetheart.

There are chains of variations
That come to my mind as I kiss
Your cheeks and sense the
Nearness f your youthful lips
Pressing onto my skin
Avoiding to touch my lips
That are for the time being still
With Anna, Aleta, Artemis looking
On with a sad expression as she
Senses that the time had come
To hand me over to Lia's lips, or
Litha's face, her budding breasts
And younger hips
Her softness in her vehemence
Her talents that stirred inside
Bursting into the open suddenly
As she comes of age
In more than physical ways
She has been maturing in her mind
Some time ago
Ad she's pretty in a demure gesture
Accepting a compliment
She likes
Yet with her temper roused
She'll change as quickly
Biting and scratching like a feral
Cat
Wanting to be her own and meet
Her destiny to face
In order to challenge the world
Head-on.
The arts.
The drawing.
And with her writing-pen

Her weapons she now wields
With skills she has acquired from
Artemisia-Anna
The other half from Nilon the Angel
And father with great love in his
Heart
In a flurry of a monologue that
Rises toward the skies and floats
Across the room
Where the young woman has
Shown her mental grit and her
Road to an early independence.

Now they have been touched by
Lia, Litha's other half of being
The poet Zinon being quiet
Shriveled into a corner of his
Erotic mind
That has been woken by Anna
Stirred-up by Artemis
And then as a great present
Handed to Lia
To be treasured.
That has woken Litha in her
Who wishes to be part of his
Desires for her
Ad become part of the loops
In her continuous mind.
Meet in mind and merge their
Bodies
That is the young one in her
Great and demanding vigour
Who'll slide upon his ageing
Carapace

His erotic scenes depicted on the
Stele of his believes
That will still rise with such an
Exuberance
To meet this unusual occasion.
Someone who loves her
Looking after her in a way
Nobody else will do
In a way some young men will
Look after Aleta
Who'll need a thunderous boost
Of loving
The glow of a younger body
That could arouse her
Take her to the edge by this want
Only youth could temporary
Provide-

The change of roles that flow from
Sister-love to lover
From mother-love to sister
Brother-love to friend and lover
Cluster of lovers that will carry-on
Endlessly to stay within the circle
Of continuity
Handed from one generation to the
Next
Such is the erotic world of Artemis and
Litha
Who would be the lucky ones
Carrying the seeds of arts and crafts
The unborn words of love that will
Flood their minds and their
Shapely bodies?

Who'll know what they would be
Who knows the fluctuating moods
Of an incidental future?

For now he has been stirred by Litha
And he has brought-up a picture in
His mind
That he'll treasure and will blow-up
To a life size 3D-poster
And he offers himself already to her
Responding to her calling
Losing his clothes already
While she will touch him and
Move him to the point of
Losing control
Until he could gather himself
To lay her down and kiss her
The way he used to kiss Aleta
But then how dews she know?
And while he continues with
Feeling lust for her
He will bring her to the boil
And raise her up and fuck her
Passed the gentle phase
Ride her extremely hard
Take his time to expose her
Raw flesh and entice her innate
Animalistic moves
Until she falls into the stream
Of continuous coming, gasping
Cries , and lustful floating with
Which she is able to suffocate
His life and snuff-out this candle
That burns deep wounds into

Her.
He cries, he shouts-out loud
In a way he could not shout ever
With Aleta, not ever with Anna
Nr with women who sprang from
The marbles of the ACROPOLIS
But now, for the first time, he
Could reach their ears and sing
And in their bodies
Vibrate the strings of their hearts
That lay so many years dormant.

Lia has made changes to his life
And she'll take his mind to boundaries
That he was never expecting to step
Across
In rising moods of confidence.
He comes.
His body writhers and his lustful cum
Is sweet
Despite being in his mind
His body just followed
Touched by her strong and willful
Hands.
And Zinon the Poet has appeared
And he cites his words in a
Continual murmur of prayers
And the music plays to it
Music he loves until his own bitter
End in lustful exhaustion...
He'll hand over his notions to Litha
Who'll carry on the arduous and
Love-filled task of a poet
A poetess, a writer who has been born

Right now at this moment.

The poet has reached through the
World of stormy seas and rough rides
The quaintness of his state of writing
And having a detached state of
Preparedness
Noting all minutely into his red and
Black notebook, his journal that deals
With LOVE and DEATH.
And now what will it be next time?
He thinks aloud.
She hopes to be still alive
And she desires to lie with him all day
As he always wished her to be
Close to him
In a wide and soft bed:
WHEN DO WE SLEEP TOGETHER?
She would ask him as he held
Her HANDS.

15
THE FIFTEENTH DAY
(Monday)

He rises somewhat aggravated
It's his inability to help, to cure
To make her well
He wishes he had some powers
Of Asklepeion just for the time to
Do the healing of her body
Bring it into harmony with her heart

And have a continued merging of
Their triad forces they did enjoy
Before
Before is always a phrase that we
Refer to
Gauging our lives against history
Against the past
And as he walks with equally vigorous
Strides towards the hill next door
The undulations of a city on the flat
The ravine, the hills of time reverberate
With lively with lively pictures in his
Mind.
That there –
The gentle sway of a breeze
In the crowns of pines
The warm-hearted look of a lonely dog
The gleaming rays of the decayed marble
Is that the way this life at present will
Be marked and thus recorded
Nameless, anonymous, stealthy
And without the slightest trace of their
Existence?
In the history of the poetess
Her work is growing to be saved and
Documented
Entered into the annals of poetic history
The papers, the periodicals
The famous who belong to a certain
Island, clan, or group of people that
Are proud to belong to.

With thoughts like these he rushes
To her and he rides the bus

The knapsack close to his feet
He guards these words like the letters
He has written from the outcries of his
Heart
The plunging of his soul into darkness
Then the emergence of it into the
Stinging brightness of daylight
That emanates from the remainder of
The temple he had assembled
Carefully with her
And fastened all his hopes and dreams
With anchors to the ivory clouds
Above that
Which falls with darkness like a cushion
And covers for their nuptial bed to be
Prepared
Their sweet fornicating cave
That has besides bitter plants
The taste of luxuriant exhilaration.

Whatever anyone places in judgement
Upon someone else
He has just never completed the truth
Of the picture he saw
Condemning matters
He himself would want to do
But has not braved the threshold of
His own realization
Or ever will.
He is adamant to see her
Even cry-out in joy he had her
WANT HER
Always wishes her to be around
And share the remainder of their lives

Together
Even with the presence of his existing
Spouse
And then her family
And then the friends they had
And so the cluster grows into this
Pyramid of bodies
That builds-up into the heavens
And he sighs as if he would ascend
Upon the entwined bodies f her
Former lovers
The soft and pliable masses that are
Friendly, smiling, hospitable, lovable
And warm-hearted towards him.
He wished Lia would be too
But then Lia is still acting like a child
Not being one any longer.
Just that Anna is not confronted with
Her will
As Anna is rather dominant
Enticed by her beauty
She cannot have a part in
Other than having given birth
To her
Ad now just as he enters her
Domain and recognizes the sounds
And scents
He is received by Anna and he holds
Her close for a few seconds
Then kisses her deep
Just as he used to
Just this time it's only for a moment
As Anna pulls away ad takes his hand
To guide him into her world

Of her present being.
Withdrawn ad pale
A ghost who lives between the walls
Of her dark reclining seat
That offers her best possible relief
She'll get at present.
He knees at her side and touches
Her – Ganymede of feelings
He breathes the air of life into her
Lifeless carapace
The sculpture he has touched on
The 'Sacred Rock'
The collection of antiquities
The one – Aphrodite of Knidos
He compared her to ad how he
Has her embedded in his mind.
A perfect match still
He kisses her body ad she comes
Temporarily alive.
Then LIA enters and he kisses her
Gently
While Lia is pressing firm kisses
Onto his cheeks
She is perhaps embarrassed to
Kiss him in front of Anna
Although Anna smiles and has
Always encouraged him to fall in
Love with her along the way
He watches Lia for years
And never had excluded her from
Any of his loving Anna
Always thought of her as his sister
Something perhaps strange.

Anna had been his Muse
Collocutor, motivator, in his poetry
And in his love for literature
Through the love
That was flowing through them
He has noted that he had still
In this corner of his heart some
Love that had been there always
For his mother.
His dear mother he loved above
All else
So much that that even his spouse
Was not much liked by her
Detested, finally abandoned as
Scorn
To be dead for her
But then he was her only son and
Most beloved
Son and father together.

And now Anna has been a lover
And sister?
Possibly a mother
His mother too
Her son she never had
And now could spoil her all and
Everything
Above all the physical love
He showers upon her most dearly
Like a lover, like a son, like a brother
And now she appears like his mother
When Lia is around
And he wishes to get the catalyst of
His body and mind between them.

He managed the mind part almost
With Lia
Who is prepared to meet him one day
As she told him
He smiles and plays the court jester
Ad Lia wonders why
As she imitates his laugh and giggles
That come a surprise to him
As he is lost for words right now
Between his want and lascivious
Desires
That Anna has already noticed
Wished as it passed her mind
Indicating to him her observant
Eyes
Pleased that he is looking after his
Spouse and she stops midway in her
Sentence
Not wanting to further entice
Knowing in her heart that she'll
Loose him.
But he needs some sexual love
That's what Anna cannot spoil him
With any longer
Nor does she enjoy it, she blurts out
Causing her additional pains.
He'll never leave her
But his eyes do rest on Lia
Carbon copy of Anna
Besides her strong will
That'll interplay with her moods
Reminding him of Anna.
Moods that could drive any young
Lover to flee, never stay as he stays

Converting into a scribe
The poet who will sit back and make
Notes, observe, ad write his story
His inner turmoil with sangfroid he
Did accuse Anna with at times
At times of his inner fire
At times of their intense love that
Deepened through their
Transcendental minds
That could merge and had the will
To merge, almost instantly
Telesthesia in automatism
Every morning
His spirit in a trance like Desnos –
The spiritual poet used to be –
So he's strongly related to Anna and
To Lia suddenly.
This is his sixth sense that Anna has
Nurtured with him
In their constant communication.

Now as she had been on a trip to
Another realm and has encountered
Loss of strength and blood
He wishes to give her his strength
Get her back onto her feet and while
She recovers
He peeks through the keyhole of
Love
And his mind with her includes her
When he's charged with autoerotic
Moods.
But such moods ad self-love only
Make him increasingly aggressive

And he hates to join the growing crowds
Of noisy music playing blasters from
Open-windowed cars and bikers that
Threaten them walking on the road
He swears at them holding-up his
Open palm against them to no avail
Some are just way beyond the road
Of rescue
Damned to be third-rate humans
Not prepared to listen to anyone
Neither priest, nor poet, either Dick
Or Doof.

For now he stalled and has this
Pressure in his guts
That rises into his procrastination
It must be hell for Anna
Despite the medication.
Her ordeal that still will come to tell
Lia about it all and then?
For some time the immediate pain
Will run through Lia's veins like
Liquid fire and burns with immediate
Rushes of refusal of Anna's ordeal
Hitting her and then her anger will
Find an outlet.
He will be here for her and kiss her
Love her as if she'd be his own child
His love and Anna's turned green
AGAIN.
Then he'll write to her some poetry
Some 'Scarlett Letters', prose, a made-up
Story, perhaps a play with words and
Lines that come to him as he closes his

EYES.
He'll draw and consumes the scenes
The imagined atmosphere, absorbs, and
Returns love that has no limits
Love that's endless
Love that has turned suddenly around
And has enclosed three women into
Its strong and caressing ARMS
Let them fall into the ABYSS of this
POET'S HEART
That's still great and pulsing
Filled with LOVE
Nourished by ANNA'S DEEP-CRIMSON
HEART.

16
THE SIXTEENTH DAY
(Tuesday)

His heart sank deeper still when
He is with her
One touch of her hands
He is aroused for her
Forever.
Magical is love
Even in a steadfast pause
Of a low-felt libidinous state
He feels love for her
Continuously
Yet, when he prepares to leave
Having had some stimulation
She will be falling asleep

While he'll write his feelings down
In a dialogue he has with her
Into the notebook she had given
Him.
It's the extension of her.
Then she gets-up and excuses herself
Accessing her neglected email folder.
Suddenly she'll turn toward him
Extends a hand
Invites him to join her
And sample some erotic pictures
Her cousin sent her about sexual
Games and love
She'll soon find them not to her
Taste – This is for men – and she's
Bored with it
With the exception of a female nude
Stretching her body with perfect
Bums
Depicted from the back
He likes it too.
After all we all have aesthetic concepts
Toward arousing nudes
We do accept turning us on –
Her, for gender love –
Him, for the love of women
Heterosexually driven within his erotic
Fantasies.

Then she stops and they study details
Of couples in lovemaking positions
That interests him
But she closes the file as it's
Mainly orientated towards a male

Erotic world.
We can look at others too
He says to her
But Anna is not in that mood.
He resigns and leaves her state of
Absent mind
Her struggle with her untimely ordeal
Feeling compassion
He holds her hands
Then hugs her gently
Not exerting the slightest pressure
And he kisses her
Enjoying the touch of her lips
The softness of her cheeks.
He touches her as she is seated
Stroking her thighs
Caressing her body
And they seem to be a couple
Known to each other for ages
Still left with some deep-seated
Tenderness in them
That they exude into each other
Time and again.

And she changes position –
He senses he has to leave
Bade farewell, find some books
Some references for his work
Literary stimulation
As if her stimulation has shifted
As is living right now between
The wall-high bookshelves in this
Reading room that stretches
Down some steps

Between the Doric colonnade of twins
And an antechamber of its high arched
Entrance.
The ceiling in a row of vaulted spaces
Painted with palmettos
Where she stood once before with him
And also sat next to him on a bench
At a row of tables
As he looked up some references for
Architect Dörpfeld.
Now he finds her again here
Just a message tells her he is in this
Sacred space they had been together
Once – he loved her here – as he loved
Her everywhere they went and stayed
Connected in body and mind.

Eratospilia – the beach that he could
Finally find although only reached with
Similar difficult walks like Llandadno
In the Cape
This is the Llandadno of Porto Rafti
With Raftis Island's natural pyramid
Rising from the deep blue waters in a
Majestic cube with the statue at its apex
Its Ben-Ben for seafarers a milestone.
He'll swim to the rocks and caves
Scouting the place he wishes Anna
To be with him here
He'll mourn in his swim and he cites
His love poems to the rocks and he
Listens to their murmuring reply
Weeping with him…
For she's not well

He could sense that
And he's away from her
He'd rather be close to her as he
Used to for 21 days on the second
Event of their meetings.

He's is looking for a sign, a signal
A bird-flight, some lonely sail
Across the undulated waves of the sea
That he swims against in search for the
Place where he may find Anna
Find his Muse, forever young and
Beautiful, forever his woman
And he wishes to *kukake* her across
Her face and her curved spinal groove
Her navel, her legs, and her pretty
Breasts...

And the poet writes:

One summer, last, you sat still
Here at Paradise Road, Starry Heights
Eros Nefeli, the seaside home
You had built for your friends and
Family.

And now as the summer of life has
Passed, the stars appear bright,
Polished diamonds with an
Areola-red moon and the warm
And sleepless nights,
The silver-plated sea, the booming
Sounds of inner calls from you.

Have I pursued you with a sameness
Of vigor as you have thought it
Worthwhile to risk all on a love that's
Worthwhile a life?

I do. And while I rest and reline
Out of my narrow
One-track mind, I travel to the
Sea, scan the shores, the sand
And coves
Perhaps I could find you
Find your footsteps there.

One summer, last, has now
Turned around for me
To be a painful ordeal of your
Earthly time, my time rendered
Sad, timid at night,
Stirred from the morning sounds
Of slippery dreams and
Befuddled spurts of the soul
That has left my tiring
Carapace.

What am I now?
I am closer to you
Than I ever was before
Online
I'm here on your shores and yet
It seems I'm further away
From you
Than before.

I'm full of love for you

But you do not wish it to be true
Rather you talk to others,
Sisters, brothers
And a host of people –
I do not even have a chance
Now any longer! Seeing you
Seeing you not! Touching you
Touching you not!
In your bed I will recline
But empty of your heart
I will sit up
Your reflection from the mirror
Does not smile, but closer to
Your eyes –
I love you instantly and quickly
Moving fast –
Closer to your face, your face,
My face –
And from the drawers a slip of
Yours, take-off your panties
For I want them close to me
Close to my inhalation,
Your taste, your scent.

But when I open my eyes
Yours are shut.
I pen the blue shutters
The night air has vanished
Into dawn
The crow has called upon...
I sit upon you, your chair
And write upon you, your skin
I stroke gently with this red
And silver pen

This transformation-style
Soft and pliable, hard at times
Like my cock.

I hid under the table
Need you here to talk back
To me, into this dialogue
That has run thin, dried-up
In the heated roll of days
I spend here alone and write
To you mere monologues.
Can't stand this stillness that
Rips me apart inside now
Vehement tortures of sex
That are autoerotic
Yet in your womb, my hands
Your eyes, my lips, your armpits
My balls, your mouth
Your finger – my anal stimulus...

I slept with her a thousand times
Perhaps even more and whatever
Thousand still to come
No thousands are enough.
While she has second thoughts and deeper
Imaginations of her terminal ill fate
I ride the wave of eroticism and intend
To keep a lookout for another girl
Just as she had in her mind for me to
Challenge another woman
That happens to be in a state of being
A potential mate.

She has suddenly collapsed mentally

And physically towards me
Not to her peers, cousins, sisters-and
Brother-in-arms, in gender, in breaking
All taboos, the most-exciting in Eros.
He is after all not only a poet, sensitive
I mind, a man of letters, he is crying
Into his lion-bushy hair that weaves
Beads of alienation around his body
While his heart is still with her
Her, he loved once, still loves, but with
That tinge of sarcasm and darkness
That flickers from her eyes at him
At times he kisses her girl, her teen
Her budding beautiful Kore
Of a daughter, still, who is an artist
In the making?
An artist he could understand perhaps
Much better as all others.

Drinking a light-golden brew and
Tossing away awkward thoughts
Let dreams survive in the midst of
Heaps of bodies in twisted moves
To a self-sell, looking for a mate.
The cock crows differently every
Time it had a hen
Cries of sexual win.
You are still everywhere cooking fish
And serving dinner
We have drinks
And take-off our clothes all of a sudden
Make love on a narrow bed.

All night the poet sits alone and writes

His letters of longing to her.
It started off usually good and then
As he wishes them to be finished
He ran out of steam
He felt just an old man, irritated
And yet inside he has detected
LOTS OF LOVE FOR HER.
Would he sacrifice something to get
Her well again?
What would it be?
His mobility, his left lung, his feet,
His cock? He'll ever sacrifices his cock!
Another game perhaps.

Another game, call it that, as we poets
Are all actors, impersonators, conjurors
Of words, court jesters to each other
More or less as we feel
Enticed or testing new waters at all times
Like now when fate has played its card
OF TAROC
That sobers our thoughts, we cry.
Sadness is a consuming illness
Nearly as bad as love
With weights on one's shoulders
That lets one crawl on the floor of
One's heart
Drown in the SEA OF ETERNITY...

There's everything in order
The immediate surroundings
The warm air, sun, and sea
With its gleaming colours
The crimson and red against the

Purple and blue
That frightens a swimmer in the
Sandy bay
Dark spots like monstrous heads
Strewn about on the bed of its rocks
Hungry demons following the
Swimmer's gentle moves.
He turns on his back and floats in a
Slight panic back to the beach
Fleeing the erotic caves of his own
Anxiety-ridden heart.
He calls on her, wanting her alive
Life never was such a puzzle
A burst mosaic of their love's
Creation
He tries feverishly to assemble back
Into its old trusted shape and fails.
He blames the wind of change that
Rattles the shutters of his blue mind
And he calls upon the gods and the
Protectors of love
Who refuse to answer back.
Then he senses defeat from their
Invisible hands
Inflicting invIsible wounds of lancing
That will kill him slowly, invisibly.

Into the Sunday morning
He can see her crystallized body
Upon the pyramid of love
That rises like a beacon from the sea
And allures with a magical call in his
Inside to swim along to her
Across the sea and its dark spots of

Frightening rocks
Reaching-out from the depth of the sea
To pull him down to join the underworld
In front of her feet
He wishes to stroke again and lie
Beside her
Even if she has become a ghost
Turning into a gleaming statue.
He'll bring her alive like Ganymede
She feels still warm to his palms
His chest, his caressing body's
Pulse.

There, as he had mastered to cross
The mystical sea
The thunder growls from its darkened
Depths and the earth will shake in a
Push and a roll that heightens the waves
Reminds of its powers and his heart
Misses a beat
He increases his motions
Finally getting ashore
Gasp and lie on the shaken pebble's
Rolling play
Lapped by the waves he flees to get to
Firmer ground
Slipping here and there
As his feet gain control
His knees suddenly strong
Having withstood collapsing
His heart cries out her name:
ANNA, ALETA, ANETHA
There on top of the pyramid
He ascends to the rambling and the

Shake
To find her gone, fainted, tumbling down
Or drowned in the open sea?
The top opens with a gash
A wound, pink and soft, gently inviting
Caressing him
Into her folds he sinks and he has
Given-up by now.
A voice that is hers tells him to stay
Calm:
TRUST ME WITH YOUR HEART.
He has given her his being and ceded
It over to her yet again.
In the purple-red chambers they meet
At last and lie together for a while
Love seems restored again
Ad sweet and willing to be consumed.
The sanctuary is firm, rock-steady and
Never in a state of fearful tension
Love rules supreme here and for
Those who carry truthful hearts.

Has he dreamed of this pyramid
The gate to the underworld?
The place we all will visit one day
If we are chosen so?
She asks him to be seated
There's no talk, no words, purely
Gestures
Which will explain and act as the
Voice.
She'll disappear and then she brings
Along her sweetheart, love, and her
Confidante, her extension of her

'OTHER LIFE'
For him to get her to know and love.
Fr many hours they converse with
This silent language
With gestures and touches and finally
Fall asleep together
Ad will wake to caressing, some love
He has never live to, never tasted
But for the first time.
When all's rather fast, hold-on to
The ghosts, he cannot and fails.
He wakes while he's swimming
Drowning, feeling tossed badly about
By an angry sea
Tired ad lying on his back
He'll try to stay afloat and make it
Back to beach and land
That lies quaint yet still filled with
Clouds of dust and smoke after it's
Mad destruction.
Now and then a tremor runs through
Beach and land
Like a tremor he felt making love to
Both women, friends, lovers, sisters,
Mothers, daughters
Two faces that loved him as if loved
By one face
Born out of each other.

The land is destroyed, burnt-out
The buildings turned to rubble
Nothing left
Hardly a soul around
A cat darts past

The birds have stopped their chirping
People silenced from their banter
Ashes everywhere.

He falls to his knees and he'll cry for
Help and loses his anger, his fright
Feeling the pain of love's separation
The passing of joys and sensations
The end of his voyage now in sight?
He'll call her name in sheer desperation
And with hope he'll wait for an answer
That never comes.
He cannot hear her words shaped by
Full lips that utter words in code
He wouldn't understand. What now?

Is it the land close to the sea
Someone uses strong words:
I FUCKING QUIT!
And then rushes away
The only couple he's seen so far
Besides her and her daughter
Himself and his son
The incomparable quartett
Mingling of young and elderly
Without any fear
To sounds of chamber music
That accompanies mother and son
Father and daughter
Sister and brother
Depicted by a seaside painter of
The occult, the spirit of the turned-up
Pyramid
The upside-down of the spinning

Wheel's axis
The blue upon the blue flows
In and out of caves
That open their bodies willingly to
The spectacle, golden showers
That lap their vaginal roses
The gigantic painting f beauty come
Alive, pregnant Gaea, luxuriant Artemis
Voluptuous Venus and swift Diana
Blown-in across the painful writhing
Of his body, taking a bite and clasp
To his skin in his climaxing terror:
ANNA, ALETA, ANETHA he shouts at
The metamorphosis of her wide-eyed
Face
The ripples of the sea that fall like
Richly curled hair
Onto the marble-roundness of her
Shoulders
Forming the fine-woven folds as her
Transparent chiton
Tussled miniature dress that swings
With the hip-accentuated steps
As she moves forward with a majestic
Gait to conquer the smoldering land
Of his body.
She cries-out in wake of her sudden lust
That is the human aspect of her being:
I come, I come, hold on tight and squeeze
And squeeze...NOW...ONCE MORE!
There will be a clashing of waves
That change to the green of olives on
The rocks and the mist that splashes
Into the falling skies to meet the army

Of the sons of Neptune and the Nymphs
Of Pegasus' efforts to slow down the acts
Of merging
The battle of the elements that
Amalgamate fire and water
Wind and air driving up the louds of red
And fiery dust
That shapes the reborn world and populates
The rising dwellings from the spunk that
Floats on top of the sea like fishing magic
Scooped ad drunk by the singed lips
Of the smoldering land.

He has created his clan and in turn
The clan has created the human clone
That grows in rapid evaporation across
The sea with love's cries
Echoing in the caves of the bay
He had been lying around, dream-like
Transparent, injected by her arrows
That found the Achilles' heel of his
Splitting body's targets
He has been living her since ancient
Times
Since the days of creation by his goddess
Of fire and swift sword
The spirit that seeps into the pores of
His mind and all elements glow in a
Celebration of light and colour that
Embraces the soft-bodied night
Like a lover.

And the poet notes:

In another morning's light
That sits behind soft-green firs
I stretch-out my hand to grab
The day
I wish to spend with you
But can do so only in my mind
Enticed by your painted face
The image on the monitor
The keyboard you've touched
Touched by me
Cannot wait to hold your hands
Even for a moment
Just a fleeting touch if fingertips
Ad opened lips
The aroused state of stealthy lovers
Surfaced just below the skin
Of their split-up lives.
But who will know?
Who will ever notice?

FIN

About the author:

Born in Eastern Austria, close to the Hungarian border, he witnessed as a young man the horrors of a nation's suppression, erupting in the Hungarian Revolution of 1956. He finished his education in art and architecture in Vienna, married and sailed for the Cape of Africa, an adventure that followed his childhood dreams. He had drawn African animals for his art classes, but the time had come to see them in their natural habitat.

Meeting a varied facet of people and cultures, working as a draughtsman in an engineering office, as an architect for a cultural centre, as a coordinator of craftsmen and professionals, he made good use of his language skills traveling throughout Southern Africa.

During a trip to Lesotho, a native artist showed him rock-paintings with their stark palimpsest outlines and with typified movements of animals and humans. It made a lasting impression on him and influenced his artistic work.

His vast collection of drawings and slides had been lost during a change of domiciles, but further studies of the art of the San-people reawakened his dormant artistic longing for expression of his art, filling sketchbooks with drawings and notepads with poetry and prose. While revisiting the capitals of Europe, he sensed the bond of art being borderless and free, reaching out across continents into the world.

During a visit to Greece, he was accepted into a circle of artists and poets, who encouraged him to continue his art and a friend introduced him to the works of famous Greek poets.

In South Africa, he joined he joined writing and poetry workshops of *Writers Write.* It was to open the floodgates of his creativity.

He decided to travel through Greece and visit its sites of antiquity, read-up on Classical mythology, and to enjoy translations of Greek poetry and prose.

He settled in 2023/14 in Klosterneuburg-Weidling. Poet Nikolaus Lenau is buried here. Franz Kafka had visited here. Their writings will always be an inspiration.

Further writings by the author, available at BoD-in their bookshop:

FIGHTING STANCE – Triangulation in Love
KING OF ICE – A poetic legend
SPLEEN OF LOVE – Zen & The Lake Moeris Adventure
THE FABRICATOR – Life & Death for a great canvas
ZORA'S MISTAKE – The potential of a hidden error.